Headline Series

No. 291   **FOREIGN POLICY ASSOCIATION**   Winter 1989–90

CANADA
Unity in Diversity

by Charles F. Doran
with Puay Tang

Cover Design: Ed Bohon $4.00

The Author

CHARLES F. DORAN is a professor of international relations and the director of the Center of Canadian Studies at The Johns Hopkins University School of Advanced International Studies. He has written articles for many distinguished journals and is the author of several books, including *Forgotten Partnership: U.S.-Canada Relations Today* (The Johns Hopkins University Press, 1984). Professor Doran was assisted in the preparation of this book by Ms. Puay Tang, a graduate student in the Center of Canadian Studies at Johns Hopkins SAIS.

The Foreign Policy Association

HEADLINE SERIES (ISSN 0017-8780) is published four times a year, Winter, Spring, Summer and Fall, by the Foreign Policy Association, Inc., 729 Seventh Ave., New York, N.Y. 10019. Chairman, Michael H. Coles; President, John W. Kiermaier; Editor in Chief, Nancy L. Hoepli; Senior Editors, Ann R. Monjo and K.M. Rohan. Subscription rates, $15.00 for 4 issues; $25.00 for 8 issues; $30.00 for 12 issues. Single copy price $4.00. Discount 25% on 10 to 99 copies; 30% on 100 to 499; 35% on 500 to 999; 40% on 1,000 or more. Payment must accompany all orders. Add $1.75 for postage. USPS #238-340. Second-class postage paid at New York, N.Y. POST-MASTER: Send address changes to HEADLINE SERIES, Foreign Policy Association, 729 Seventh Ave., New York, N.Y. 10019. Copyright 1990 by Foreign Policy Association. Composed and printed at Science Press, Ephrata, Pennsylvania. Winter 1989/90.

Library of Congress Catalog Card No. 89-81592
ISBN 0-87124-131-5

Ties that Chafe

For most Americans, relating to Canada is like talking to one's neighbor across a backyard fence. From the Canadian perspective, the problem is that Americans sometimes forget about the existence of the fence. Canadians seem so similar. Yet their political preferences, social values and cultural composition often are at odds with those of mainstream America. This puzzles Americans, even on occasion infuriates them. Why should a country so close geographically, so complementary in its traditions and heritage, so apparently familiar on the basis of individual citizen contacts, act in ways that appear from time to time so perverse—indeed, that appear so non-American?

The answer of course is that Canadians are not Americans, nor in preference or behavior do they want to become American. Yet they are enormously affected by everything done in the United States. Moreover, they measure themselves against a nation that has a population almost 10 times larger than Canada's and is the

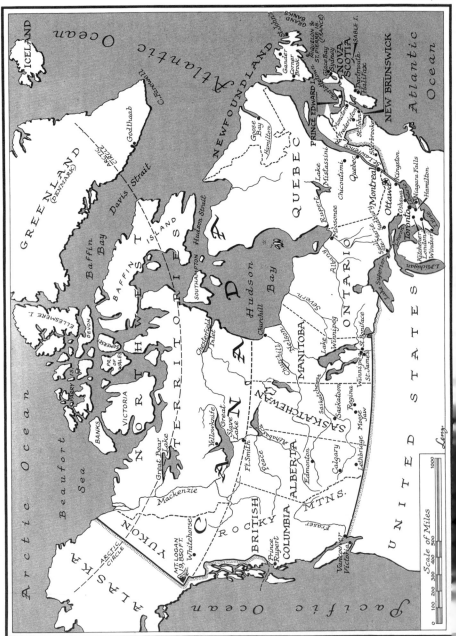

focal point of much of the world's political and commercial activity. Because of the very proximity, size differential, and the apparent societal congruence of the two countries, Canada seems to spend an inordinate amount of time convincing itself, and the world, that it is not the United States. In reality, Canada has a unique identity, and is different because it wants to be different. Canada is an act of social will over circumstance.

Unity in diversity characterizes a nation that from its colonial origins arose out of a compact between two "founding peoples," one French-speaking, the other English-speaking. This reality, perhaps more than any other, sets Canada apart from the United States. Although both Canada and the United States share a British colonial heritage, the United States forcibly rebelled against British "tyranny"; Canada clung to that heritage, never denouncing its relationship with Britain as oppressive and, indeed, transforming the relationship into orderliness, justice and prosperity. But the Canada that arose from British benevolence was a diverse and fractionated country.

If Sweden is a land of small towns, and France is a land of small shops, Canada is surely a land of small communities. Each region of Canada is defined. Newfoundland, the last province to join the confederation, is proudly parochial. The Maritimes—New Brunswick, Nova Scotia and Prince Edward Island—look eastward. Halifax, Nova Scotia, may be the only city in North America where the citizens read about local politics in London or Washington, D.C., with as much interest as they do about their own politics in Ottawa. Quebec is the great heartland of the French language and culture. Ontario, the richest and most populous province, sometimes confuses itself with the interests of Canada as a whole ("If it's good for Ontario. . ."). The vast Prairie Provinces—Alberta, Saskatchewan and Manitoba— share a climate, cultural outlook and a common struggle with nature that reminds one of life in Montana or North Dakota. British Columbia, "the land beyond the mountains," is westward-looking and as rich a source of new ideas and innovation for Canada as California is for the United States.

But Canadian unity has a North-South dimension as well.

Prime Minister John G. Diefenbaker (1957–63), for example, heralded the idea of the "True North, strong and free," yet in reality the Canada known by most of its citizens is a narrow band scarcely 100 miles wide, adjacent to the U.S. border. The mythology of the great North, and of a "Northern people," is strong and inspirational. But imagine a country 100 miles wide and 30 times as long, occupied by concentrations of population and industry at widely spaced intervals. The reality of location and habitat for Canada is far more restricted and fragile even than that depicted by the mythological struggles to survive in the far North.

This is the country that most Canadians see and that most Americans seldom comprehend. As a widely dispersed "border people," Canadians have had to rely more than most on the government to assist in providing transportation and communications. Government has been the instrument to overcome or to circumvent diversity. Yet at the same time, Canadian society demands that its diversity be preserved. There are no myths of homogenization, or of assimilation, to promote cohesion. Unity must spring directly from a social contract that guarantees the authenticity and separateness of the various parts of Canada, parts that together, somehow, must be retained in the whole.

Toronto, Canada's most populous city and the capital of Ontario, lies just across from the United States on Lake Ontario, within a few miles of Chicago, Detroit, Cleveland and Buffalo— all competitors and partners within the great North American heartland. Toronto, however, is different. Its streets are clean. There are no slums. Despite occasional racial tensions, the city is harmonious. The murder rate does not inhibit a nighttime stroll.

Within the Toronto city limits, more than 60 languages are spoken and offered in one place or another within the city school system. English is the lingua franca in Toronto, yet cultural, ethnic and linguistic diversity are preserved through the application of public tax dollars. "New Canadians" are beginning to outnumber "old Canadians," yet the laws of the land somehow continue to promise the preservation, not the amalgamation, of societal diversity.

Canada's Importance to the United States

Canada's importance to its southern neighbor is apparent in many subtle ways, ranging from the contributions that Canadian artists and businesspeople make to North American preeminence, to the access that Canada provides to some of the most exciting vacation locales in the world. Canada's significance at the national level, however, is much more clearly evident in the contributions that the country makes to trade and commerce and to common security interests within Norad (North American Aerospace Defense Command) and NATO (North Atlantic Treaty Organization).

The United States trades more with the province of Ontario than with any single country, including Japan. As much trade occurs between the United States and Canada as between the United States and the entire European Community. The commercial and trading link between Canada and the United States has generated an enormous single trading area.

Some 80 percent of Canada's foreign trade is with the United States. About 20 percent of U.S. goods and services traded abroad goes to Canada. The disparity in relative trade levels results from the different size and national output of the two countries. Although Canada comprises a larger geographic territory than the United States, its population and its gross national product (GNP) are roughly one tenth those of the United States. Yet regardless of these disparities, in practice each country is bound closely to the other.

This tight interdependence raises several problems for Canada. Having such a large concentration of its foreign trade with a single partner, Canada is highly vulnerable to every shock and policy adjustment emanating from the other side of the border. The impact is unavoidable, whether a U.S. policy initiative is aimed at Canada or whether it is responding to some third-party development.

Even Canada's achievements pose a problem. In trading terms, its success is measured by a surplus in manufactured goods that has fluctuated but has favored Canada for much of the postwar period. Although most governments would envy Canada the size and persistence of its trade surplus in manufactured goods with the United States, Canadian government officials worry that possible envy concerning this surplus could lead to retaliatory measures.

In fact, much of the trade surplus represents receipts from a single item, the export of automobiles and automobile parts. This is covered by the terms of the 1965 special Automotive Agreement (Auto Pact) between Canada and the United States that provides for free trade between the two nations in cars, trucks and auto parts. (The Auto Pact is enshrined in the Free Trade Agreement—FTA—of 1988.) When energy prices are down and consumers buy larger cars, Canada benefits because the Big Three automobile companies in Canada in recent years have tended to produce the larger models. In such periods, the Auto Pact seems to augment a Canadian trade surplus in the balance of payments. What U.S. critics of the Canadian trade surplus sometimes forget is that it is offset by a U.S. surplus in the current-account balance which includes so-called invisibles—services, interest payments to the United States, insurance premiums and the like. Since the end of World War II the United States has had a current-account surplus in all but a handful of years.

Furthermore, Canada is to some extent locked into interdependence with its giant trading partner to the south. Canada knows that if it tried to diversify its markets, it would do so at the cost of industrial development unless present global trade patterns changed. No other trading partner imports such a high proportion of Canadian manufactures and semimanufactures as the United States. Although such trading partners as Japan and Western Europe would increase their commerce with Canada, they would do so only on the basis of purchasing higher volumes of Canadian raw materials (and then, of course, only at or below the prevailing world price for these materials). Thus, for Canada to try to diversify away from the North American marketplace would mean substituting the possible advantage of lesser dependence for the clear disadvantage of less industrial development. Very few Canadians, whether labor union members or corporate managers, would settle for this kind of negative exchange.

Top U.S. Trade Partners in 1988

in billions of U.S. dollars

	Exports	Imports	Total trade
CANADA	**$70.9**	**$80.9**	**$151.8**
Japan	37.7	89.8	127.5
Mexico	20.6	23.3	43.9
West Germany	14.3	26.5	40.8
Taiwan	12.1	24.8	36.9
Britain	18.4	18.0	36.4

Source: Department of Commerce

High levels of interdependence have also aroused Canadian sensitivity with regard to the process of trade, most of which is conducted through intracorporate exchanges between large multinationals and their branches in Canada. Although the level of foreign ownership has declined somewhat, between 35 and 50 percent (depending on the definition) of Canada's industrial base is either owned or controlled by foreign companies. Approximately 80 percent of these are located in the United States. (The corresponding figure for foreign ownership of the U.S. industrial base is less than 5 percent, with Canadians holding only a small, though increasing, fraction of this percentage.) Canadian sensitivity about foreign ownership, mollified considerably by the probusiness attitude of Brian Mulroney's government when it first came to office in 1984, is understandable, if at the same time misplaced and counterproductive. The extent of the jobs created and the taxes generated in Canada through intracorporate exchanges would be no greater if the branch plants were Canadian-owned or -controlled. Moreover, worries about the extent of foreign ownership reduced the inflow of foreign capital in the 1980s at the very time when it was most needed.

It should also be noted here that heavy interdependence with Canada has caused some anxiety for U.S. business as well. Some 20 percent of total U.S. foreign investment is located in a single country, Canada. Although not as concentrated as trade with Canada, this is still a significant slice of foreign investment, considering the overall high levels of foreign ownership in Canada and the edginess of some members of the Canadian elite and public about the foreign role in the Canadian economy.

Despite these tensions, however, trade and commercial interdependence between the United States and Canada have contributed to the achievement of prosperity levels unrealized in many other areas of the global economy. Although partly attributable to the economies of scale that the large North American market affords, this prosperity is principally owing to the comparatively unfettered nature of both economies, guided according to market principles. Even so, the two countries have periodically attempted to create a more-formalized free-trade area in order to reduce tariff and nontariff barriers between them and to try to remove the shocks and uncertainties in those areas of the trading relationship in which each side is most vulnerable and in which each has historically suffered from the other's actions (for Canada, trade; for the United States, investment).

Efforts to establish freer Canada-U.S. trade have made difficult progress, beginning with the Reciprocity Treaty of 1854 (prior to Canadian confederation in 1867). The treaty allowed some commodities and raw materials to move across the border tariff-free. The end of the Civil War in the United States, however, marked the political demise of the low-tariff, agricultural South, and the U.S. government listened to its northern merchants who opposed the treaty's renewal. In 1911 free trade was again tried and failed, bringing down with it the government of Prime Minister Sir Wilfrid Laurier (1896–1911). In 1948, a free-trade agreement, which had been quietly engineered by bureaucrats on both sides of the border, was killed at the last moment by Canadian Prime Minister William Lyon Mackenzie King, who apparently considered it too risky in political terms.

Thus, Canada's importance to the United States as a trading

partner was especially celebrated on January 1, 1989, when the Canada-U.S. Free Trade Agreement finally came into effect, acknowledging the existence of a free-trade area that had been forming for more than a century. This area is presided over by two separate and sovereign federal governments that have accepted the responsibility of ensuring that the host of state, provincial and other governmental jurisdictions within their boundaries carry out the agreement's provisions. Hence, the monumentality of an agreement in an undertaking so long elusive.

NATO and Common Security Goals

Perhaps the best way to appreciate the importance of Canada to the United States—and the United States to Canada— in security terms is to imagine in its place a country with hostile intent. It is precisely upon this basis of mutuality of security interest and concern that the borders between the two countries have remained open and demilitarized. Ever since the Rush-Bagot executive agreement, signed in 1817, the Great Lakes have been maintained as a neutral waterway upon which warships do not travel and passage is unimpeded. This record of openness is truly remarkable, a record among nations that hyperbole scarcely distorts.

Several institutions have emerged that have increasingly reinforced bilateral defense relations. One is the Permanent Joint Board on Defense (PJBD), established in 1940. Arising out of the Ogdensburg Agreement, in which Prime Minister Mackenzie King and President Franklin Delano Roosevelt (1933-45) decided to coordinate their countries' efforts on behalf of a joint defense of North American interests during World War II, the PJBD has remained a valued colloquium for defense matters. It is a common ground where military officers from each country can familiarize themselves with the perspectives of the other country and establish ties that serve well the interests of their own polity.

From an operational point of view, NATO is the fulcrum of defense coordination for both Canada and the United States. Canada shares with all other NATO members the same military interest in collective security and a strong and united Western Europe. In addition, however, Canada is unique in its highly developed political interest in NATO membership—membership that is more important as a political counterweight for Canada than for any other member.

In the absence of NATO, Canada would be isolated on the North American continent, despite its participation in the British Commonwealth and its French equivalent, la Francophonie, with the United States as its sole effective ally. Although Canadian and U.S. security interests are complementary, they are not always identical in either North American or global terms. Within NATO, Canada is usually able to find support among like-thinking states for a view counter to that of the senior partner, the United States, and such opposition is made respectable by membership in a common alliance. All members, large or small, have a "seat at the table" and contribute to the making and implementation of collective strategy. Of course, alliance membership also has its obligations, as Prime Minister Pierre Elliott Trudeau (1968–79; 1980–84) discovered when he allowed the testing of cruise missiles on Canadian territory in spite of Canadian public opinion that was for the most part lukewarm to hostile. Thus, NATO provides the Canadian government with constructive flexibility that enables it to display foreign policy autonomy to an electorate that is sometimes overly nationalistic.

With regard to collective military defense, Canada is taking a more active role pursuant to the Mulroney government's 1987 defense white paper that called for a reassessment of the NATO commitment. After the Trudeau government's 1968–69 decision to halve Canada's military deployments in Europe to 2,500, Canada stationed approximately this number of highly trained troops, including tank units and air cover, on the central front in West Germany. In accordance with the white paper,[1*] Canada is now attempting to strengthen and upgrade the quality of its troop commitment there, which had increased to 4,200 by 1985–86.

The decision to concentrate on the central front involved a significant shift of strategic emphasis away from the effort to

---

*See footnotes on page 64.

bolster the defense of Norway. Expertise regarding how to fight and to supply troops in polar conditions is not easily acquired. Canada believed that it could specialize in a type of defense that would also serve the security of its own northern territories. Specialization would also increase the significance of Canada's contribution to NATO defense, since no other nation could match the quality and intensity of Canadian training in the art of northern defense.

The Case Against Military Specialization

Ultimately, the decision against specialization in northern defense and against directly assisting Norway was made at the cabinet level. The issue, however, was widely debated throughout the Department of National Defense (DND) and centered around four concerns.

First, the so-called CAST (Canadian Air/Sea Transportable) Brigade, located in North America, was not easily deployable in Norway. Not only would it have been difficult to move troops and equipment quickly to Europe in response to a crisis, but defensive operations would have been greatly complicated by the fact that heavy equipment, such as artillery, and supplies were not in place. Transport would probably have depended not on Canadian, but U.S., aircraft—if not already otherwise deployed—and this reliance was, if nothing else, anathema to many Canadian military planners. Thus CAST was a deployment on paper and therefore a contradiction.

Second, Norway did not make things easier for Canada. Because of its internal political situation, Norway's leftist political parties were able to demand that no foreign government be permitted to station equipment and troops on Norwegian territory. Similarly, the government on occasion seemed to believe that preparation for adequate defense of its northern reaches would invite the Soviets to augment their military activity on the Norwegian border. A NATO consensus on whether that judgment is valid—or rather, whether the Soviet Union will increasingly regard the Norwegian Sea as a corridor to the south—has not been reached.

Third, Canada has always been leery of military specialization, however much this might enhance its contribution to collective defense. Canadian military organization is based squarely on the concept that Canada must maintain a kernel force representing all branches of the military and capable, by virtue of its training and leadership, of being expanded into a full-sized armed force on short notice. Thus specialization as to function is as incongruous for Canada as it is for other countries possessing much larger standing capability.

Fourth, West Germany strongly argued that Canadian forces were needed where the threat was actually greatest—on the central front. Given this threat, and the greater sense of having troops in fighting position when needed, instead of awaiting transport, the rationale for a focus on West Germany prevailed over a northern-flank strategy. Intra-alliance politics, mediated but scarcely controlled by Washington, ultimately determined the direction of the new Canadian strategic emphasis.

Whether Canada will be able to pursue all aspects of the white paper's proposals concerning the reinforcement of its contribution to the central front remains to be seen, especially since some of the recommendations do not seem internally consistent. In particular, the plan to purchase 10 to 12 nuclear-powered submarines to operate under the Arctic ice cap, which was subsequently scrapped, tended to relegate all other aspects of the Mulroney defense policy to a backseat. Yet the basic conclusion with respect to Canadian involvement in NATO is that Ottawa continues to regard NATO as the principal focus of its participation in collective defense.

North American Aerospace Defense

Norad, the third Canada-U.S. defense arrangement, was established in 1957 despite Canada's traditional inclination to limit highly visible defense cooperation with the United States and to downplay proposals for forward Arctic-based deployments. The cold war had compelled Canada to take a different approach, and the Joint Statement on Defense Cooperation, signed in 1947, expressly encouraged mutual cooperation regarding air, naval and military facilities. Thus Norad emerged as a bilateral institution for the defense of North American airspace. Although Canada periodically sought to associate Norad with NATO, the fact that NATO's greater military vulnerability was in parts of Western Europe and that Europeans had no interest in contributing directly to North American defense meant that Norad would become what the United States had more or less intended.

Headquartered near Colorado Springs, Colorado, and composed of a number of regional commands, Norad enjoyed an interval of central importance when the bomber threat was paramount. As intercontinental ballistic missiles (ICBMs) and sea-launched ballistic missiles (SLBMs) became more important, however, Norad's functions became less critical. Less a retaliatory capability, Norad became more an instrument for warning and attack assessment, as well as a peacetime surveillance mechanism for unidentified aircraft.

Although Norad at first was criticized by some Canadians—both in terms of its value as a defense instrument and for the subordinate role they believed it assigned to Canada—it remains an important institution, characterized by close cooperation between U.S. and Canadian military officers. In organizational terms, the commander in chief (Cincnorad) has always been an American and the deputy commander, a Canadian. The enormous authority for North American defense is inherent in both positions, as the deputy commander would assume charge if the commander in chief were unable for any reason to reach Norad headquarters. This responsibility may be declined, however, upon the decision of the Canadian prime minister, in which case all functions would be performed by Americans. This option emerged after some Canadians criticized their air force officers for acting in advance of a decision by the prime minister by supporting the U.S. alert during the Cuban missile crisis of 1962.

Norad has continued to adapt its defensive functions as military realities have changed, modernizing in response, most significantly, to a renewed potential Soviet bomber threat employing cruise missiles, and upgrading its surveillance and command and control functions through a combination of F-15 fighters, airborne warning and control (AWAC) aircraft and over-the-horizon backscatter radars (OTH-B).

With the increase in military space activities, Canada-U.S. differences have arisen over Norad's appropriate defense functions. In 1982 the United States established a Space Command to integrate aspects of these activities and air defense outside Norad. Yet Canadians are skeptical of the U.S. Strategic Defense Initiative (SDI, or "star wars") and of certain elements of the U.S. defense doctrine, and some have renewed their call for a withdrawal from bilateral defense functions of which they disapprove. Nevertheless, Norad is unlikely to collapse either because of disagreements between Canadians and Americans concerning its functions or because of unilateral actions by either government. Both countries recognize its necessity and importance.

Norad provides Canada with several distinct security-related benefits. It supplies Canada with a voice in planning and operations. It ensures that Canada will be a part of the defense not just of its own territory but of all North America. It also means that breakthroughs in space technology and military communications are more likely to include a Canadian component. If Canada did not participate in Norad, the United States would be forced to shoulder air- and space-based defense alone. Yet at the same time it would be able to pursue a defense apart from whatever countervailing influence Canada might wish to bring to bear. For all these reasons, Canada is unlikely to find withdrawal from Norad to be in its national interest.

Similarly, the United States values the contribution Canada has made to the cost of upgrading facilities, such as the new land-based radar systems, and to their day-to-day operation and maintenance. Moreover, access to Canadian and U.S. airspace must be mutual to be effective. Coordination of the North American defense effort is the only plausible way to protect the sovereignty of each country while achieving the highest possible level of defense preparedness. Despite variations over time in strategic emphasis, Norad will continue to play a critical role in many facets of continental defense.

Canada Is *Different*

However much Canadians seem like Americans, and however much Canada and the United States appear alike when set against the rest of the world, Canada is different. Canadian attitudes toward aspects of defense underscore this fact. Although similarities do exist, Canada is a nation formed along such sharply defined regional and cultural lines that it is as internally diverse as it is collectively unlike any other country. Generalizations about Canada are bound to be wrong, since regional realities vary so greatly. Within Canada's immense expanse are distinct groups of people with contrasting provincial interests and communal outlooks that manifest themselves in creative tensions rather than uniformity. The political process is expected to arbitrate among all of the competing demands—demands that Canadians often articulate forcefully. Yet Canada's strength is the unity that it finds in diversity.

Canada's importance to the United States—especially evident in the areas of trade/commerce and defense/security—was symbolized in both the Reagan and Bush Administrations by the choice of Ottawa as the locus of the first foreign trip by a newly elected President. As economics rises on the foreign affairs agenda of most countries today, Canada's position as the largest trading partner of the United States becomes more salient for U.S. politics. Similarly, as defense matters become more complex technologically, and more diffuse and regionally sensitive in global terms, Canada's place as partner and neighbor is more greatly appreciated. The psychology of Canada-U.S. relations, under these circumstances of interdependence and intervulnerability, requires further assessment. Such an evaluation can only be made in the context of the evolution of Canada and its unique political institutions.

From Confederation to
Political Maturity

Canadian historical writing reflects two distinct viewpoints. One centers around the transfer of British political, constitutional and legal institutions to Canada and their subsequent adaptation to Canadian conditions. The other focuses on French-Canadian themes and seldom highlights the larger Canadian scene. Rather, it stresses the way in which French Canadians retained their identity while adapting to British political institutions. Emphasizing the exploitation of French-speaking Canadians by their English-speaking counterparts, it portrays a history of animosity and antagonism between the two groups. Another frequent theme is the Quiet Revolution of the early 1960s—the turning point for French Canadians, when Quebec, which has always been predominantly French in cultural outlook, became a modern, secular, urban society.

English and French rivalry on the North American continent dates back to the original competition for territorial control. Boundaries between English-held and French-held territory were often disputed. In 1713 the Treaty of Utrecht attempted to force the French out of the Hudson Bay region, Newfoundland and Acadia (Nova Scotia), but they remained firmly entrenched in Acadia and along the St. Lawrence to Montreal.

When the Seven Years' War broke out in Europe, the war between France and Britain crossed the ocean to Canadian territory. In the summer of 1759 the British laid siege to the city of Quebec and defeated the French in a decisive battle at the Plains of Abraham. The Treaty of Paris in 1763, by which France ceded to Britain all claims to Acadia, Cape Breton and all territories east of the Mississippi (except for the islands of St. Pierre and Miquelon in the Gulf of St. Lawrence), signaled the demise of French power and the beginning of English dominance in Canada. French Canadians bitterly refer to this event as the Conquest.

As the Union Jack was hoisted triumphantly over Canada, the government faced the task of dealing with *les Canadiens*—some 60,000 strong. Early attempts at assimilation were stated in coercive terms, compelling the French to give up their language and religion if they wanted to participate in the political life of the new nation. Such Anglicization actually reflected British law, which prevented Roman Catholics from holding office, but it is little wonder that to this day French Canadians view assimilation and Anglicization as threats to their identity.

To a great degree, however, this was simply a declaratory policy, and many early governors were highly sympathetic to the French Canadians and anxious to gain their confidence. No doubt they also realized that good relations with the French Canadians would be valuable if overtures (by French or Americans) were made on behalf of rebellion. Thus, in 1774 the British Parliament passed the Quebec Act promising French Canadians the right to hold public office without taking the anti-Catholic oaths still required in Britain. The act, which acknowledged the legitimate rights of the French Canadians in many ways, is upheld by French Canadians as a sort of Magna Carta that safeguarded their rights and enabled them to survive as a distinct people in Canada and North America. As will be seen, this act became one of the most controversial pieces of legislation in Canadian history.

In 1791 the Province of Quebec (old Canada) was divided into Upper Canada (later Ontario), which was predominantly English-speaking, and Lower Canada (later Quebec), with a larger French-speaking population. The Canadian duality, part of the diversity of modern-day Canada, thus came into existence.

In 1812 Britain and the United States were at war again, and the Canadian provinces (Quebec and Ontario) found themselves on the front line. U.S. soldiers invaded, their leaders confident that Britain's war with Napoleon would prevent the arrival of reinforcement troops. But the Americans overestimated their own capability, and with their defeat came a lasting sense of separateness between the people of Canada and the United States and the inculcation of anti-Americanism into the Canadian consciousness. "The War," as all Canadians refer to it, marked the last time foreign troops encroached on Canadian soil.

Internal Strife

With foreign threats out of the way, the Canadian provinces had a greater opportunity to manage their exasperating regional loyalties and intransigent differences. Yet between 1812 and 1867, the provinces, unable to unite around a common purpose or theme, proceeded to develop in different directions that reflected their separate economies and that enhanced parochial outlooks and loyalties. Furthermore, the provinces were not politically joined, but were merely constituent parts of the British Empire.

In 1837 the two largest provinces, English Upper Canada and French Lower Canada, erupted in armed internal rebellions after a period of extreme tension brought on by severe economic, social and political problems. After the rebellions, tensions continued between French- and English-speaking Canadians, as Lower Canada again identified itself as a conquered people, dominated by an English-speaking oligarchy. Cognizant of this animosity and frustrated by the suffocating localism of the provinces, Lord John George Lambton Durham, the governor-general, recommended in 1839 the unification of Upper and Lower Canada and proposed internal self-government to foster the union's cohesion. The two were joined in the single Province of Canada by the Act of Union in 1840. The governor-general, however, was somewhat mistaken in thinking that Canada would be easier to govern once the French-speaking Canadians became the minority in the larger union.

By 1864 it was clear that the French- and English-speaking populations of the Province of Canada were too dissimilar to work harmoniously in one legislature in which each group was supposed to regulate the affairs of the other. An alternative that quickly gained support was a federation government, whereby each province would be managed by its own local legislature and federal issues would be handled by a general legislature. This proposal complemented well the growing interest in the West as an outlet for agricultural and industrial products. With the greater use of railways, agricultural surplus and products could be transported to new markets. By the 1860s, however, the Province of Canada had nearly reached the limits of agricultural growth within its existing territory. Becoming part of a larger union, linked by a transcontinental railway, could both provide a way out of the political cul-de-sac and enable Canada to have a West of its own in the face of American Manifest Destiny.

In the aftermath of the American Civil War and the defeat of the agricultural South, the United States was no longer so enthusiastic about free trade with Canada. The industrial North wanted protectionism, and the United States failed to renew the Reciprocity Treaty of 1854 with Canada. This reality, combined with some anxiety about the size of the U.S. Army and the American government's intentions, created an atmosphere in Canada conducive to confederation.

The decision to dissolve the Province of Canada and recast Quebec, Ontario and the Atlantic Provinces into a confederal structure was less visionary than expedient. The intent was to create a political structure that would continue as a self-governing entity within the British Empire and benefit through territorial expansion, rather than to found an independent nation. Thus, under the British North America Act, the Dominion of Canada came into existence in 1867, consisting of the four provinces of Ontario, Quebec, New Brunswick and Nova Scotia. Manitoba, to the west of Ontario, was admitted in 1870; British Columbia, on the Pacific Coast, was admitted in 1871; and Prince Edward Island, on the Atlantic, in 1873. Canada, a new nation north of the 49th parallel, had finally begun to overcome its disparateness.

The Early Prime Ministers: Nation-Building

The first decade of the Canadian confederation was a time of trial and despair. The depression of 1873 hit Canada particularly severely, and this economic gloom served only to sharpen the many existing tensions within the new nation. Resentments deepened, as it seemed that whatever benefits the confederation had brought had accrued primarily to the central provinces. The Maritimes felt neglected; British Columbia was enraged that the railway it had been promised in accordance with its entry into the confederation was overdue. The problem of building unity in the midst of regional disparity was as impressive as it has been enduring.

National unity was the challenge, and it was on the platform of implementing a "national policy" that Sir John A. Macdonald, the Conservative first prime minister of the Dominion of Canada, was voted back into office in 1878. (He had been forced to resign the position earlier due to a scandal involving the Pacific Railway.) Macdonald's national policy was a broadly based program of economic development that involved raising tariffs to protectionist levels to preserve Canadian markets for Canadian industries. Yet this "materialistic policy of Bigness,"[2] as John Dales has aptly described it, to prevent Canadians from being the proverbial hewers of wood and drawers of water, did not forward the common cause of national unity. In fact, it encouraged regional disparities among industrial central Canada, agricultural western Canada, and underdeveloped, ignored eastern Canada. Strains created by an influx of multiethnic settlers, the concerns of native Indians, and the rekindling of French-Canadian nationalism combined to sweep the Conservative party out of power in 1896.

The economic climate had dramatically improved by the time Prime Minister Laurier of the Liberal party assumed power in the summer of 1896. But heightened controversy over the rights of French-speaking Canadians confronted the new prime minister. In 1896 New Brunswick and Manitoba adopted judicial measures that vigorously challenged the concept of duality supposedly guaranteed by the Quebec Act and by provisions in the British North America Act. Now Quebec was demanding a federal system of coordinate powers in place of a guarantee limited to cultural rights and dependent on central government protection.

Macdonald's philosophy of governing, based on the idea of a strong central government, was replaced by the Laurier emphasis on local independence and provincial rights within a federal system. Thus the duality of the Canadian union, exemplified by yet limited in the confederation, reappeared. Now each province was armed with its own powers; each was inward-looking, with Quebec still "nationalist" in temper.

Other divisions beset the Laurier government, as French-Canadian nationalists attacked the prime minister for approving (reluctantly, in fact) a small Canadian navy to be put under British naval command in time of emergency. Many English-speaking Canadians believed just as strongly that Canada's interests would be best served by a close partnership with Britain. At the same time, the perennial issue of trade relations with the United States, which began long before confederation, returned to haunt Laurier. Even though Macdonald had placed Canada on a protectionist course, partly in response to U.S. protectionism, free trade with the Americans had been a goal of many politicians since the mid-nineteenth century. Yet when Laurier agreed to President William Howard Taft's (1909–13) proposal for lowering tariffs on a broad range of items, Canadians vigorously objected that this was the first step toward annexation by the United States. The slogan, "No truck nor trade with the Yankees," helped bring the Laurier government down in 1911. Riding into office on a theme of Canadian nationalism, the government of Sir Robert Laird Borden (1911–20) will perhaps best be remembered for its struggles over conscription during World War I and an upsurge of nationalist fervor in Quebec.

Prime Minister Mackenzie King and the Liberals came to

power in 1921, and, except for the period 1930–35, he remained in office until 1948—an unprecedented length of service for a prime minister. King was a strange man, who found solace in his diary, his dogs and spiritualism. But he was a conciliator, and his political leadership was premised on discussion, consultation, caution and allegiance to Laurier's ideals.

As King entered the forefront of Canadian politics, the country was groping its way toward a changed status in the international community. King advanced this trend during the 1920s and 1930s. For example, he refused the British government military aid during the Chanak crisis in Turkey on the grounds that he could make no promise of international involvement, especially military involvement, before consulting the Canadian Parliament. In 1923 Canada, for the first time, signed a treaty without an accompanying British signature. At the Imperial Conference in 1926 the leaders of Britain and the Dominion formally recognized Canada's changed status within the Commonwealth (this term now replaced Empire) by declaring that the dominions enjoyed equal status with Britain. This statement was translated into law by the Statute of Westminster in 1931.

King was also a good student of history, and when conscription, which had divided Canada along French- and English-speaking lines in 1917, reemerged as a national issue in 1939, he was determined to keep the country unified and his party's power intact. Distant from the world's trouble spots, Canada had managed for some time to avoid entanglement in collective security measures emanating from the League of Nations. When war broke out in Europe in 1939, however, Canada found itself obliged to come to Britain's aid. King, true to his middle-of-the-road, ambiguous style, managed to avert a showdown between Quebec and the rest of the country by his well-known formula, "not necessarily conscription, but conscription if necessary." Conscription for home duty was introduced in 1940, but conscription for overseas duty did not begin until 1944. Fortunately for the Liberal party, the war ended before many conscripts could see action.

Intersecting issues of defense were two important bilateral

agreements that King had signed with the United States. One established the Permanent Joint Board on Defense. The other was the Hyde Park Declaration (1941), which was intended to facilitate defense-related trade between the two countries and set the stage for the Defense Production Sharing Agreement of 1959, still in effect today.

King left a legacy that was important though not ostentatious. Unified and still capable of being returned to office, the Liberal party had kept the country united as well. King selected a French-speaking Canadian to serve as secretary of state for external affairs, Louis S. St. Laurent, who succeeded him as party leader and as prime minister in 1948. He held the post until 1957. Canadians were satisfied with Liberal hegemony. Liberalism seemed to offer the country what it needed.

Recent Governments: Prosperity and Crisis

St. Laurent, a lawyer who had had little experience in political organization before being elected prime minister, was not particularly interested in learning about administration. He relegated these tasks to his lieutenants, especially Clarence Decatur Howe. However, St. Laurent was bright, exceptionally clear-minded, and was a "master of the cabinet, and of the civil servants who appeared before it."[3] As King's secretary of state for external affairs, St. Laurent had delivered the epochal Gray Lectures, "The Foundations of Canadian Policy in World Affairs," in which he enunciated several basic principles that have since guided Canada's foreign relations. The first principle stated that Canada's external policies must not destroy the country's unity. The other guiding principles included a commitment to political liberty, the rule of law, and willingness to accept international responsibilities.

A man of moderate policies, St. Laurent was also a virtuoso in the art of maneuver, and he used his talents to preserve national unity and pave the way for more active and continuous Canadian participation in world affairs. When Quebec refused to join the single national income tax system proposed by the federal government, St. Laurent agreed to exempt Quebec in return for some concessions. Although this compromise in effect secured for Quebec a position of distinctiveness—fulfilling the sort of nationalist aspiration on the part of the provinces consistently denounced by St. Laurent—the prime minister deemed it necessary and by it he successfully defused the situation. Through his astuteness, his vision and his determination to keep Canada tightly unified, St. Laurent launched Canada onto the international scene. It was the St. Laurent government that undertook the delicate task of persuading the Canadian public to accept the idea of an Atlantic alliance (NATO). By 1956 Canada had distinguished itself as a "middle power" par excellence by helping to resolve the Suez Canal crisis through the genesis of a multilateral peacekeeping force to manage international conflict. Under the leadership of the Liberal party, Canada had also achieved further territorial consolidation, with Newfoundland joining the confederation in 1949.

Diefenbaker, 'the Chief'

St. Laurent was succeeded by the Progressive Conservative party leader from Saskatchewan, Mr. Diefenbaker, "the Chief," in 1957. Under the Diefenbaker administration the internal harmony and overall consistency that had prevailed in the St. Laurent years seriously eroded. It was a time of contentious politics, reflecting both the external environment and Diefenbaker's personality. Strong-minded and suspicious of the Liberal-dominated Department of External Affairs, the prime minister insisted on defining foreign policies personally.

Diefenbaker's foreign and domestic policies were marked by dogmatism and high principle. He and External Affairs Minister Howard Green labored hard to bring about global disarmament. Stridently denouncing South Africa's repugnant apartheid policies, Diefenbaker refused to give any assurances that he would vote in favor of South Africa's application to reenter the Commonwealth. At home he offered a bill of rights, and in 1960 his Act for the Recognition and Protection of Human Rights and Fundamental Freedoms received royal assent. He supplied extensive agricultural assistance to western Canada, increased unemployment benefits, doubled grants to universities, and arranged for Quebec universities to begin receiving dominion funds as well.

Emotionally supportive of the British connection, Diefenbaker was distressed about the closer integration of the Canadian and U.S. economies. He advocated several measures to divert trade from the U.S. market to the British market, but the dilution came to nothing. In fact, more oil and manufactured goods moved southward, following the lines of comparative advantage. The Canadian dollar depreciated to such an extent that it became derisively known as the Diefendollar. Not only did the Diefenbaker government suffer from bad management and the dollar debacle, but it also engendered bad feelings by making unpopular decisions on defense policy. For instance, it canceled the AVRO Arrow, a supersonic fighter plane, and in the process laid off 14,000 workers. Although such a decision may have been inevitable, many observers believe that the Canadian aeronautics and avionics industry was set back because of the government's policy. Bitter feelings swept through the Conservative party and across the country when the government approved deployment of the Honest John missiles, intended to hold atomic warheads. At the same time, Diefenbaker's ambivalence about allowing nuclear weapons on Canadian soil did not make for strong, clear-cut policy in this area of critical concern. The prime minister's refusal to place Canada's Norad force on alert during the Cuban missile crisis, for fear of exacerbating tensions, helped push Canada's defense policies into disarray, while, to quote Robert Bothwell, preserving "its nuclear virginity intact."[4]

Within the Chief's own party, disorder followed upon indecisiveness and confusion, broken promises and "Diefenbabble,"[5] prompting even senior members to question their leader. The party weakened, Canada's allies infuriated, and national defense debilitated, Diefenbaker was voted out of office and eventually forced out as leader of the Conservative party.

Mike Pearson

The changing of the guard saw the Liberals back in power under Lester (Mike) B. Pearson (1963–68), who had been St.

Laurent's secretary of state for external affairs from 1948 to 1957. More of a diplomat than an administrator, however, Pearson avoided setting agendas and was prone to ambiguity, thus proving unable to convey an image of coherence in his government.

The new prime minister also lacked extensive knowledge of the Quebec problem, although as a clever politician he surrounded himself with French-Canadian political leaders. Upon their well-considered advice, Pearson promulgated a doctrine that amounted to cooperative federalism. By promoting "the greatest possible constitutional decentralization and. . .special recognition of the French Fact and the rights of French-speaking Canadians in confederation,"[6] unity would be strengthened. Yet in 1963, by which time the membership of other ethnic groups had grown significantly, Pearson's attempts to repair French-English divisions led to fragmentation on other fronts. With the announced formation of the 10-member Royal Commission on Bilingualism and Biculturalism, which included only two representatives from ethnic minority groups, western Canada hastened to denounce the commission's mandate.

Pearson's policies in other areas also proved to be controversial. In the politico-military sphere, Pearson implemented his electoral pledge to acquire nuclear weapons, a clear about-face for Canada that incurred much opposition even from fellow Liberals. At the same time, he resisted increasing the defense budget and staunchly gave priority to peacekeeping, for which he had won the Nobel Peace Prize in connection with the 1956 Suez Crisis. Pearson's foreign policy record was not without success, including the stabilization of Canada-U.S. relations. But what Pearson won in diplomacy he lost in his articulation of policy, which was too often ambivalent. For example, in a speech at Temple University he openly denounced the U.S. bombing of North Vietnam, yet later apologized to President Lyndon B. Johnson. Pearson had promised Canadians that he would publish his correspondence with Johnson concerning Vietnam, and he suffered much embarrassment when the President refused to permit this. Similarly, Pearson's Quebec policy of cooperative federalism and accommodation gave way to a harder line after 1965. Toward the end of the

1960s, Pearson realized that he had accomplished all that he could and that it was time for him to retire from public life. In 1967 he announced his intention to resign as Liberal party leader.

Trudeau

In 1968 Canada's justice minister under Pearson, Pierre Elliott Trudeau, acceded to the positions of party leader and prime minister. Described as confident, aloof, intellectual, charming and yet abrasive, with methods that were more confrontational than conciliatory, Trudeau was a new kind of leader. As prime minister, his raison d'être was national unity and he clearly tolerated only a minimum recognition of Quebec's separateness.

The greatest challenge Trudeau faced was posed by the Parti Québécois, under René Lévesque, who once served with Trudeau on the staff of the magazine *Cité Libre*. Lévesque was a nationalist—in the Quebec sense—and called for separation of the province from the federation. Trudeau traversed the country, including Quebec, arguing in intellectual and emotional terms against the separatist movement and for a "just society" that would continue to reflect unity in diversity. Undoubtedly, a large percentage of Quebec's electorate wanted to safeguard and highlight Quebec's culture; however, most proved too fearful of the economic consequences of isolation to see Lévesque's plan through to completion. In a May 1980 referendum only 42 percent of the province's voters supported Lévesque in his attempt to secure a mandate to negotiate sovereignty-association, that is, political independence with continued economic association with the rest of Canada. Nevertheless, progress was achieved on behalf of the rights of French Canadians and their representation at senior levels in the civil service.

In 1970 Trudeau initiated a thorough review of Canada's foreign policy. In *Foreign Policy for Canadians*,[7] Trudeau laid out his new conceptual framework, according top priority to domestic issues and economic prosperity and correspondingly low importance to security. He also downgraded Canada-U.S. relations, which would remain strained throughout his administration.

Under Trudeau's leadership Canada began to emerge as a more independent player on the international scene. Convinced that the cold war was over and that Canada should rethink the nature of its alliance relationships, Trudeau reduced Canada's manpower contribution to NATO by half. For this he was loudly criticized by his allies as well as by the domestic opposition, but his decision fitted comfortably into Canada's long tradition of antimilitarism. By recognizing the People's Republic of China in 1970, he intended both to demonstrate to a world audience that the international system was changing and to strike an independent posture from that of the United States. He devoted great effort to strengthening a "North-South dialogue," believing also that development assistance to the Third World, in addition to environmental and arms control measures, would best serve his nation's interests. Throughout his term as prime minister, Trudeau systematically and publicly identified the conceptual bases of Canadian foreign policy, highlighting Canada's relevance in a changing international system even as he reestablished the guidelines for the formulation and implementation of Canadian foreign policy.

In the area of economic policy, Trudeau pursued a strategy intended to move Canada in the opposite direction from its historical dependence on the U.S. economy. This "third option," introduced in 1972 by Secretary of State for External Affairs Mitchell W. Sharp, was a comprehensive, long-range strategy to develop and strengthen the Canadian economy, primarily through aggressive diversification of markets. Canada would substitute expansion of markets in Europe, Asia and the Pacific Rim, including Latin America, for growth in the U.S. market. The option failed in its major goal of reducing Canadian economic dependency on U.S. trade.

Nevertheless, Trudeau was determined to enhance Canada's control of its economy, and toward this end he established organizations which would enable Canada to better direct its economic future. He called for the formation of the Foreign Investment Review Agency (FIRA), which began operations in 1974, screening takeovers and transfers of ownership from abroad and directing foreign investment into new enterprises and areas. U.S. investors—the major foreign direct investors in Canada— loudly protested the measure. Trudeau also took steps to strengthen the Canadian energy industry. In 1973 he called for the formation of the national petroleum company, PetroCan, to arrange for oil imports, work the oil sands of Alberta, and explore for conventional oil and gas. In other words, Canada was to have its own company that would coexist with the multinationals.

More political than economic in its conception, the National Energy Program (NEP) formed in 1980 was designed to "Canadianize" the Canadian energy industry by ensuring that 50 percent of the country's oil and natural gas assets were Canadian-owned or -controlled by 1990. It provided production subsidies and priced Canadian oil for domestic consumption below world price levels. Yet instead of increasing energy self-sufficiency, the NEP threw the energy industry into a depression. Moreover, its political impact was damaging for confederation. Alienated Alberta retaliated by reducing production. It was only under the next government—with the dismantling of most of the NEP —that the Canadian energy industry was able to recover.

'Patriating' the Constitution

Finally, on a more successful note, the Trudeau government sought to "patriate" Canada's constitution from Westminster, where the British monarch's sanction was still theoretically invoked. Canada, by then 113 years old, was the only major country not to have custodianship of its own constitution. Patriation involved not so much a transfer of power from Britain to Canada as difficult judgments concerning the powers of the provinces. Again Trudeau traveled throughout the country, garnering support for his idea. When he could not persuade by intellectual argument, he appealed to emotion. With only Quebec dissenting, he achieved his goal in 1982.

Thus, from 1968 to 1984, Canada followed an impressive course under the leadership of Trudeau. Though he lost the prime ministership to Joe Clark of the Progressive Conservatives in 1979, the loss was quickly overturned the following year. Clark had turned the tide against the Liberals, showing their vulnerabilities. But the inexperience of the Conservatives also became evident when the government was brought down by a loss-of-confidence motion in Parliament after the introduction of an economically plausible but politically risky federal budget. To quote a well-known Canadian journalist, Allan Fotheringham, "Trudeau [is] the most remarkable Canadian of his generation; he did more than anyone to make this country sit up and take notice. Well, back to the mundane men."[8]

Mulroney and the Politics of Maturation

One would not describe the leader of the subsequent Conservative government, Brian Mulroney, who succeeded the brief Liberal administration of John N. Turner (June 10, 1984 to September 17, 1984) as mundane. A successful labor lawyer from Quebec, he was determined to correct the mistakes that he thought the Liberals had committed. Mulroney's Conservative agenda included restoring the Canada-U.S. relationship, increasing Canada's defense contribution to NATO, and repairing cleavages between the federal government and the provinces. Yet Mulroney had inherited a mature nation, despite its problems—a prosperous Canada with a significant business community and market, a Canada less afflicted by a sense of inferiority and more confident of its foreign policy direction.

The Mulroney government, no doubt remembering the premature defeat of the Conservative government under Clark, cautiously proceeded to address the tough domestic and foreign issues confronting Canada. It began slowly, soliciting the public's views on foreign policy issues before setting policy. The parliamentary committee dispatched on this mission presented its conclusions in a foreign policy green paper published in 1985 under the title *Competitiveness and Security: Directions for Canada's International Relations.*

On the basis of the green paper's conclusions, Mulroney was able to establish two important policies. The paper had revealed that the Canadian public was not enthusiastic about the U.S. strategic defense initiative, which, as announced by President

Ronald Reagan, would create a very expensive, highly complicated, multitiered defensive shield. Admittedly, most of the witnesses before the parliamentary committee were critical of defense policy in general. But the Mulroney government "interpreted" their responses and decided that although Canadian companies would be free to participate in SDI, the Canadian government, like its European counterparts, would not officially embrace SDI. In addition, Mulroney used the green paper as a public relations medium to support the notion of a free-trade agreement with the United States. Cognizant of the importance of the U.S. market to Canada, he attempted to ease the way for a more satisfactory trade relationship. Even before the green paper was released, Mulroney, with his highly personal political style, had encouraged the image of friendship between him and President Reagan at the so-called Shamrock summit in Quebec and fostered the idea that Canada could count on this friendship. Friendship would be translated into progress toward improved bilateral trade relations.

Mulroney's government also successfully straddled a potential foreign policy conflict with the United States over Canada's territorial rights to the Northwest Passage. Canadians had long held that the entire Arctic North all the way to the Pole (including the Northwest Passage), within designated longitudes, was Canadian territory and that it therefore had the right to regulate its waters. Just as firmly, the United States had always contended that the Northwest Passage was international waters. The incompatibility of these viewpoints had already been demonstrated when the U.S. oil tanker *Manhattan* had tried to cross the Northwest Passage, prompting the Trudeau government to pass the Arctic Waters Pollution Prevention Act of 1970, which laid extensive environmental claims 100 nautical miles out from Canadian shores.

In 1985 the voyage of the *Polar Sea*, a U.S. icebreaker, through the Northwest Passage again enraged the Canadian public, which demanded that Canada assert its sovereignty. Ironically, Canada and the United States had quietly worked out the terms for the voyage, establishing that it would neither be considered a legal precedent for passage nor require a formal diplomatic request for passage, thus justifying the principle of Canadian sovereignty. Nevertheless, Canadian public opinion (and the party opposition) forced Ottawa to respond, and it did so by making more-extensive territorial claims in the Arctic. Indeed, it is only within the context of the debate over Arctic sovereignty that one can understand Canada's controversial proposal to purchase 10 to 12 nuclear-powered submarines capable of operating under the Arctic ice cap. Ultimately, U.S. decisionmaking at the highest level helped smooth tensions on the sovereignty issue. However, the United States has perhaps not yet fully recognized how sensitive sovereignty matters are for Canada and how they impinge in complex ways upon continental defense.

On the domestic side, the Mulroney government rapidly dismantled the highly criticized National Energy Program, which had scared off foreign investment and damaged relations with the West—in particular, the United States. It dropped or reduced differential oil-pricing and production subsidies. In truth, the NEP had backfired, not because of foreign commercial opposition but because of world recession and a downturn in world oil prices. A reduction in foreign ownership and control in the Canadian oil industry was occurring in any case. Thus, Mulroney saved PetroCan and sent a strong signal of his intentions regarding renewed Canadian economic growth and prosperity.

In sum, the vulnerability that Canada feels in its foreign policy is reflected in the political evolution of the state and its institutions. In Canada, foreign policy is often calculated to reinforce domestic policy. The perceived fragility of Canadian society and identity, as expressed at various times by its prime ministers, is a catalyst for the way in which Canadians choose to be governed. Accustomed to different forms of democracy, outsiders sometimes fail to comprehend the complex norms and countervailing pressures operating within the Canadian governmental system. Unity emerges out of diversity when this system is perceived by Canadians to be operating fairly and efficiently.

The Distribution of Power

In order to understand the development and conduct of policy in Canada, it is important to see how power is distributed in the Canadian system of government. A simple identification of authority will show that the British monarch is the head of state; the governor-general (a Canadian), the monarch's representative in Canada; and the prime minister, the head of government. The latter's unique responsibilities and powers, as Canada's national leader, derive from a highly complex framework of authority. A member of the cabinet, he is much more than first among equals: ". . . from first to last the prime minister was first in fact as in form—to the end he remained the one indispensable man in government."[9]

The prime minister is also party leader; he is selected by a party convention and elected by the people in his riding, or electoral district. Thus, he owes his position to the grass roots of the party, not to the party caucus in Parliament or to the cabinet—a fact that gives him great room to maneuver. The personality of candidates for the office sometimes becomes the focal point of an election when the divisions in Canadian society prevent each political party from uniting on major issues. If the prime minister is challenged by his cabinet or party caucus, he can reinforce his authority by taking his case to the public that voted for **him** rather than for a particular policy or program.

The prime minister's office has a virtual monopoly of power within Parliament, especially evident when the governing party has a sizable majority. Although cabinet ministers, who are appointed by the prime minister, run the government with the help of the bureaucracy, the prime minister can use various strategies, including demoting or dismissing a cabinet minister, to ensure that his point of view prevails in any policy dispute.

The prime minister holds equally great power over the bureaucracy, including its senior members, regardless of their years of experience and knowledge of government. The bureaucracy may on unusual occasions dominate individual ministers, but not the prime minister. He has broad powers, without the restraints of, say, the U.S. Civil Service Commission or the Treasury, to make appointments to the top levels of the public services. These appointees can frustrate the bureaucracy's influence over policy.

With this power base, the prime minister controls the policy agenda through the Privy Council Office, which centralizes and coordinates policy formulation. As supreme policy coordinator, he has access through this office to information not easily available to his colleagues. This advantage, plus the fact that he appoints the members and assigns the tasks of cabinet committees—which are extensively used—makes the prime minister the best-informed person in the cabinet.

Finally, the prime minister is the only person who can ask the governor-general of Canada to dissolve Parliament and call an election. His power is indeed considerable, but it must not be misconstrued that the prime minister is free from constraints. Ultimately, his success depends on his ability to balance the demands and expectations of his ministers and the electorate.

The Cabinet

The cabinet has a notable degree of independence and flexibility. No document defines its responsibilities; it is not specifically mentioned or described in any law. Yet the cabinet is the center and mainspring of Canadian government, the source of policy and legislative pronouncements. It is here that quasi-judicial, political and administrative decisions are made. Because the prime minister and the cabinet normally control a majority in Parliament, they control the lawmaking machinery. At times the cabinet takes actions that have the effect of altering or going beyond the original intent of Parliament. Acting as governor-in-council, it can proclaim only part of a law that has been passed by Parliament, thus delaying the implementation of other parts.

The fact that the cabinet has not been constitutionally defined enhances the prime minister's flexibility as well. For example, because no rule states whether cabinet ministers must be members of Parliament, the prime minister may select ministers outside of Parliament, although it is understood that those selected will find seats as soon as possible. Since 1867 this has happened more than 20 times.

The cabinet's independence also derives from the comparative secrecy in which the group operates. Neither the opposition parties nor the backbenchers in the governing party are privy to enough information to check governmental action. Strict party discipline also encourages this independence since the government's majority in Parliament is not threatened by crossover voting. Furthermore, parliamentary committees, compared with those of the U.S. Congress, are weak, small and poorly staffed. Although the 1984 McGrath Commission recommended that parliamentary committees be given more resources and consultative participation, the governing party still has no obligation to bring issues before these committees for review. Thus, despite more-apparent consultation, the cabinet effectively controls Parliament—at least when a majority government is in power.

Ministers, in addition to participating in the cabinet, must also be alert to the political consequences of policy proposals made by officials in their own departments and throughout the entire government. They must frequently appear before the public and keep in touch with opinion throughout the country to avoid serious criticism of their departments. They must also look after the needs of the constituents they represent in Parliament. In short, Canadian cabinet ministers, unlike their counterparts south of the border, are both politicians and parliamentarians.

Three Major Political Parties

Prime ministers and cabinet ministers are drawn from the government party, one of the three major federal parties. The Canadian party system traces its origins to the preconfederation legislative assemblies.[10] From an inchoate system dependent on local patronage and the governor's powers, it has coalesced and developed into a stable system including the Progressive Conservative party (PCP), the Liberal party and the New Democratic party (NDP). There are also provincial parties, such as the Parti Qúebécois and the Social Credit party of British Columbia, which reflect, more so than the national parties, bicultural, geographic or class cleavages.

The Progressive Conservatives are often characterized as politically right of center, the Liberals at the center and the NDP left of center. Yet no such clear distinctions exist. Only the NDP has a pronounced ideological perspective, and within each party there are left- and right-wing elements. Especially since the Tory election victory of November 21, 1988, it would be more accurate to characterize the Liberals and, in particular, the Progressive Conservatives, as status quo coalition parties.

The Progressive Conservative party stands essentially for less government intervention, laissez-faire economics and business liberalism. Yet it was Macdonald's Conservatives who instituted protectionist tariffs over the loud protestations of Liberals; the Liberal Laurier who was defeated because he favored free trade, or reciprocity, as it was then known; and the arch-Conservative Prime Minister Richard B. Bennett (1930–35) who proposed the Canadian "New Deal" in the 1930s. In reality, Canadian conservatism tends to possess an element of "Red Toryism"—a paternalistic concern for the public welfare and an occasional

Canadian Prime Minister Brian Mulroney and President Ronald Reagan at the 1986 two-day summit in Washington, D.C.

preference for strong government intervention in the marketplace.

Canadian Liberals are not the equivalent of U.S. liberal Democrats. Canadian "liberalism" is less individualistic, more inclined toward state intervention in the economy, and more ready to implement a variety of social welfare measures. The Liberal party does not stand for society's opposition to big business. It claims to represent no particular group but **all** people. The Liberal view is that "true political progress is marked by. . .the reconciliation of classes, and the promotion of the general interest above all particular interests."[11] Frank Underhill, a well-known authority on the Liberal party, commented that it monopolized the center of the political spectrum and spread out so far both to the left and right that it overshadowed the opposition groups and rendered them less effective. The Conservative party, to a lesser degree, has also adopted a broad-based platform. No fundamental principle distinguishes the policies of one party from the other, and their differences are more likely than not to reflect the personal philosophy of a prime minister or changes in the domestic and international climate.

The NDP grew out of the Cooperative Commonwealth Federation (CCF) as a farmers' movement intended to assuage the Prairie Provinces' discontent. The CCF was a socialist movement that also drew support from the urban working class, university intellectuals and gospel preachers. Formed in the midst of the Great Depression, the CCF was one of the first parties in Canadian history to build an organization with a cadre of leaders and a clear philosophy, and it needed this coherence to offer a sustained challenge to the two major parties. With postwar prosperity, the CCF realized that its platform was too narrow, and in 1961 it formally merged with the labor movement to establish the New Democratic party. The NDP, today considered the second major opposition party, claims to be the advocate of the people and embraces either a socialist or social-democratic philosophy. Strong among intellectuals in Canada, and with a popular base in the agrarian west and in Ontario ridings with a heavy labor presence, the NDP adds excitement and an occasional touch of radicalism to Canadian politics. Although one may wonder whether its affiliation with the trade unions will make the NDP more conservative, its largest significance lies in its "innovator role" in opening up new areas of legislation. By providing an alternative to the two coalition parties, the NDP challenges them and the electorate.

The Judiciary: Charter of Rights and Freedoms

Canada is governed by two systems of law. Although all 10 provinces share the same criminal law statutes, Quebec's civil law is based on the Napoleonic Code, and all other provinces have adopted the traditional Anglo-Saxon common law. The Canadian judiciary operates on three levels—the provincial courts, the federal courts, and the Supreme Court of Canada. All Canadian courts were established by provincial legislatures or the federal Parliament, since the British North America Act made no provision for a court system. Consequently, no court is protected by the constitution from legislative change. The judiciary, however, is an independent branch of government, free from external political coercion by the prime minister and the cabinet. It also has the right to declare a statute to be *ultra vires*, that is, beyond the jurisdiction of the legislature that passed it, thereby enabling the courts to thwart legislative and executive decisions of which they disapprove. Furthermore, the rules of interpretation established by the courts can often dull a statute's impact.

Constitutional adjudication in Canada today is at a turning point. In the past, even when the 1960 Canadian Bill of Rights was enacted, judicial interpretation of the constitutional powers of government did not amend or affect the British North America Act itself. The Charter of Rights and Freedoms, which is part of the Constitution Act of 1982, has significantly broadened the focus of judicial review, bringing the constitutional rights of individuals under the purview of the courts. The charter bestows rights on Canadians as individuals, and these rights are secure from the power of either the provincial or federal governments. Although the charter affords federal or provincial lawmakers latitude to write legislation in such a way that it is exempt from some of the charter's most important provisions, governments that exercise this power run a risk of not getting reelected.

Judicial interpretation of the charter, by putting certain policies beyond the legislative reach of the provincial and federal governments, will lead to court vetoes of legislation and of executive actions. It may also force governments to follow judicial orders. Although Parliament still makes the laws—and the charter permits no one, not even the courts, to replace Parliament—the judiciary certainly has a new role: to enforce the constitution as the highest law among all those who govern and are governed.

Bilingualism

Since confederation, Canada's single most visible cleavage has been the French-English division of society. Highly conscious of cultural differences, French Canadians have sought to maintain and deepen their separation from English-speaking Canadians. Examples range from their simple identification as *Canadiens* to the separatist movement in the province of Quebec, which posed a severe challenge to national unity in the mid-1970s.

Quebec's Quiet Revolution, beginning in 1960, captured the imagination and attention of people beyond Canada, particularly the French. It transformed a rural culture dependent on a very conservative Catholic Church into a modern, industrial and secular society. Quebec in every sense enjoyed a renaissance and heralded the revolution by the slogan *Maîtres chez nous* (masters in our own house). Reflecting the belief that this required control over the economic and cultural life of the province, French Canadians worked to gain a more influential role in business. Politically, they continued to pursue a separate status and forced Ottawa's hand by seeking to establish their own diplomatic ties and agreements with France. Many Ottawa officials, in fact, believed that independence for Quebec was inevitable unless the federal government asserted its right as sole representative of French Canada abroad and preserved the bicultural character of Canada's international personality. The Pearson government therefore moved quickly to create "umbrella agreements" with foreign powers, whereby provinces could reach agreements with foreign governments but only under the protection and signature of covering federal legislation. Ottawa hoped in this way to legitimize Quebec's dealings with France while reaffirming Quebec's status as a province no more privileged than any other.

Not surprisingly, the president of France, Charles de Gaulle, did not take kindly to this measure. He recognized in Quebec the spirit of boldness and courage needed to earn "a continued place in the sun." Accordingly, he continually irritated the Canadian government, snubbing the Canadian ambassador to France, demanding that Canadian troops leave French soil, and refusing to attend the war memorial ceremonies at Vimy Ridge in northern France, which Canadians captured from the Germans in World War I, thus repudiating past ties. The crowning insult came during his 1967 visit to Montreal, when from the Hôtel de

Ville (city hall) he dramatically threw his hands up and proclaimed to the 10,000 cheering French Canadians, *"Vive le Qúebec! Vive le Qúebec Libre! Vive le Canada Français! Vive la France!"* To English-speaking Canadians, this was heresy; to many French Canadians inside and outside Quebec, it was not amusing; to many in France, it was an outrageous intrusion. Many Québécois, of course, loved it.

Official recognition of the distinctiveness of Quebec and the Canadiens, with their hard-fought right to equal if not better treatment, was theoretically to be assured by the Meech Lake accord drawn up in 1987. Yet constitutional amendments alone are unlikely to change the conflicting views on the bilingual question. It should also be noted that there is tension between French-speaking Canadians **outside** Quebec and the rest of the English-speaking majority (excluding the non-Anglo English-speaking immigrants). Although less emotionally "nationalistic" than some Québécois and more "Canadian," they nevertheless share the same feelings of exploitation and subordination and remember the "conquest" just as bitterly as the Québécois. For their part, English Canadians resent what they believe to be "reverse discrimination" in civil service jobs. Faced with the reality of "two solitudes" within a single nation, Canada will continue to structure its official doctrine to accommodate its bilingual society. The effort will remain an enduring feature of Canadian unity in diversity.

Federal-Provincial Relations and Regionalism

Few subjects are as crucial to an understanding of the Canadian political system as the study of federal-provincial relations and regionalism. Given Canada's diverse and regionally fragmented society, it is not surprising that federal-provincial diplomacy and territorial competition have preoccupied every administration. Political and institutional arrangements intended to alleviate this tension often exacerbate rivalries by displeasing one group or another.

Fiscal relations in the federal-provincial arena are at the very core of the Canadian political process, and an examination of these relations will show, probably better than any other set of institutions, the vicissitudes of Canadian federalism.

For example, in 1867 the British North America Act vested primary responsibility for raising money, directly or indirectly, in the federal government. The provinces, however, were authorized to raise revenue by direct taxation, for example, from fees for licenses and permits and municipal taxes on real estate and personal property. Federal revenue typically went toward public works, the development and management of railways, and national defense. Provincial revenues were used for education, public welfare and transportation. By the 1930s the provinces had developed and expanded their range of services to the point where decreasing revenues could not support such necessary services as health and education. Conversely, the federal share of the costs of government had declined significantly. Thus, the relationship between the federal government, which had the preeminent ability to raise money, and the provinces, which had the preeminent obligation to spend money, had to be reexamined.

In the wake of the Great Depression and World War II, Canada adopted several fiscal measures to correct this imbalance. These included the expansion of the provincial tax base and the introduction of equalization payments, by which richer provinces, under the auspices of the federal government, in effect would make grants to poorer provinces in order to raise levels of public service to consistent standards. Cognizant that socioeconomic issues can both promote territorial rivalries and exert a powerful nationalizing influence, Canada's federal government has devoted much time and money to resolving such matters. Yet fiscal relations do not exist in isolation, as the introduction of equalization payments showed. Provinces demanded greater powers vis-à-vis the central government in accordance with their assumption of a much larger share of the cost of government. Nowhere has the importance of territorial competition in Canada been more evident than in the search for a new constitutional order.

This search, however, has only tangentially addressed a primary cause of territorial conflict—the lack of adequate regional representation within the institutions of the national government. In the absence of such representation, territorial concerns have been channeled almost exclusively through provincial governments. As a result, premiers have become powerful national regional spokesmen, less checked and challenged than members of the U.S. Congress and more important than most governors.

To help manage regionalism, the federal government instituted the annual First Ministers' Conference, which provides a forum where the provincial premiers can meet with the prime minister to express their differences and present their demands. Many intergovernmental conferences are held each year at the senior levels of the bureaucracy. But the basic problem of ineffective regional representation inside the federal government remains, and the provinces continue to depend on the tightly integrated network of federal-provincial consultative bodies within the federal system.

Meech Lake Accord

Negotiation, once an occasional mechanism for resolving differences, has become a continuing feature of relations among the provinces. Furthermore, despite the turnover in representatives of the federal government, a commitment to bargain, seek agreement, and compromise is typical in federal-provincial relations as well. The Meech Lake accord of 1987 demonstrated this willingness, as it attempted to correct the lack of regional representation within the federal government and to address a primary area of contention between provincial and federal government—Canada's bicultural character. By conferring the status of "distinct society" on Quebec, the accord brought Quebec into Canada's constitution, delivering what the federalist forces had promised during the 1980 Quebec referendum on sovereignty-association.

In seeking to increase regional representation, the accord ran the risk of further decentralizing the federal government. For example, the accord gave provinces an absolute veto over constitutional amendments affecting Senate reform, the extension of existing provinces and the creation of new provinces. Provinces were to be allowed to opt out of shared-cost programs (a distinctive feature of Canada's fiscal federalism), which meant that provinces could disregard "nationally accepted standards." Furthermore, by allowing premiers to submit lists of candidates for Supreme Court judgeships, the accord could result in a judicial bias toward provincial rights. More significant, a lessening of federal authority and expansion of provincial jurisdiction risked increasing tension in an already tenuous relationship between the provinces and the central government. Similarly, allowing provinces to select their own senators, subject to appointment by the prime minister, would in the view of some critics be tantamount to creating a Senate of provincial-government appointees. According to some constitutional experts and federalists, this would be the equivalent of putting much of the federal government under provincial trusteeship. Ultimately, although the Meech Lake accord provided for improved regional representation, it also threatened to open up a range of new problems for Canada. Given the controversy over the Meech Lake accord, there was some doubt that it would receive the support necessary by the June 23, 1990, deadline for enactment.

In short, Canadian government is designed to complement a society in which diversity is the rule. According to John Meisel, a Queens University political scientist, when society is reasonably homogeneous and cohesive, governmental institutions can be decentralized, but when society is fragmented and diverse, governmental institutions must be centralized. Ottawa has a very centralized form of government at the federal level. It shares fewer powers with the federal Parliament than it does with the provinces. Unity emerges from the very federal-provincial relations that have evolved over the years. The manner in which the provinces conduct themselves, even as they preserve diversity in the society, remains the key to future governmental unity.

Free Trade, Defense
and Acid Rain

A measure of the distance between novice and "old hand" in matters Canadian is the latter's implicit understanding of the psychology of Canada-U.S. relations. Because Canada lies astride the continent and adjacent to principal U.S. cities, most Canadians are closer to a major U.S. metropolitan area than to Ottawa. They feel overwhelmed. Canadians for the most part try to do everything Americans do (often with great success) in spite of fewer numbers. It is little wonder that such a strategy leads to occasional frustration.

In Canada-U.S. bilateral visits, which have become annual events, the Canadian prime minister must be seen by his countrymen to "get something" from the U.S. President. At the very least he must present a challenge. Even if there were nothing on the agenda to talk about (and that has never happened), the Canadian head of government must appear to push the U.S. head of state for change. The more real the benefits and the more visible the dialogue, the more successful the visit from the viewpoint of the Canadian citizen and press. From the U.S.

perspective, the index of skill is how to manage such an exchange without "giving away the homestead."

Alternatively, when the United States has a grievance with Canada, it invariably downplays and disguises it as an "irritation." This does not mean, however, that behind the closed doors of 24 Sussex Drive, the prime minister's residence, the United States fails to convey the message with vigor. On the contrary, some of the discussions between counterparts at various levels of government are very frank. For the United States the "medium" is not the "message." The medium is chosen very carefully so that the message is the message.

Over the years the Canada-U.S. dialogue has developed its own rules. Good relations between prime minister and President, and between the secretary of state for external affairs and the U.S. secretary of state may be regarded as extremely important to the smooth functioning of the relationship.

By world standards, Canada-U.S. relations must be regarded as a paragon of harmony. This is partly because Americans and Canadians understand each other so well; partly because each respects the limits of the dialogue. Canadians temporize; Americans "take the long view." Fundamentally, neither the American nor the Canadian people allow their governments to go too far in upsetting a relationship upon which so much depends. They know it is unique, and they want to keep it that way.

Canada-U.S. Free Trade

The Canada-U.S. Free Trade Agreement finally came into formal effect on January 1, 1989. After so many decades of failure to acknowledge the emergence of a growing free-trade area, the feat of agreement fittingly took place on the heels of an election campaign in Canada that focused upon free trade as the principal issue. John Turner, the Liberal party candidate, said he was not against free trade but that he was against this particular agreement because it was too encompassing and yet too weak to secure Canadian access to the U.S. market. Prime Minister Mulroney used his office to articulate the merits of free trade while pointing out that on six months' notice the agreement could be canceled by either government if its terms became too arduous. Returned as a majority government in November 1988, the Progressive Conservatives lost no time in putting the agreement into effect. It is interesting to speculate about why the Canadian people finally opted for a free-trade agreement with the United States.

Behind the Canadian free-trade decision was a kind of "if-you-can't-beat-'em-join-'em" mentality. Under Prime Minister Trudeau, the Liberal government had espoused the so-called third-option approach to trade. The object was to diversify trade partners, notably by developing trade with European countries and Japan, but, as described earlier, the third option failed. Meanwhile, competition from outside North America, principally from Japan and the newly industrializing countries, was becoming more intense. Canada was also becoming increasingly wealthy and more confident of itself politically and culturally. Indeed, the last Trudeau government initiated free-trade talks on specific categories of products with the United States that became the forerunner of the actual comprehensive talks. (The protectionist threat from the United States, which could cost Canada access to the U.S. market, was very frightening to Canadians.)

All of these factors tended to converge and persuaded the Canadian government and electorate of the need for a historic break with Canadian wariness about too close an association with the United States. Rather than risk losing access to the world's largest single market, Canadians decided to acknowledge formally that they were already an important part of that market. A Canada-U.S. free-trade area was born.

Under the FTA, by the end of this century, tariffs on both sides of the border will have been eliminated, most in phased reductions. Since Canadian tariffs were on average 9 percent at the time of signature of the agreement, and U.S. tariffs 5 percent, this commitment to tariff reduction says something about Canadian resolve.

Since the FTA created a free-trade area and not a common market, no common external tariff exists. Rather, each government determines what type of external barriers it enforces.

Rules-of-origin provisions prevent the transshipment of goods from outside, through one country to the other. The rule of thumb is that imported parts must be altered or improved sufficiently to be traded as an entirely new product with a different tariff classification to get FTA duty treatment. For the auto trade not covered by the Auto Pact, the rule is 50 percent North American content. The FTA will reduce customs problems on goods indigenous to Canada and the United States, but it may well increase the difficulty of evaluating goods imported into North America.

Provisions of the FTA regarding major sectors of trade and commerce are:

First: Providers of services from one country to another in the future are to be accorded "national treatment," that is, to be treated as well as domestic companies "in like circumstances." There are also more-detailed arrangements for telecommunications and some other services. A possibly important qualification in the Canada-U.S. context is that if a state or province discriminates against the other parts of its own country on a service item, it can discriminate against the other country as well. (Except for the latter qualification, this agreement on services could become a model for a multilateral trade pact.)

Second: Since the trade in automobiles and automobile parts makes up such a large share of the total value of Canada-U.S. trade, the continuation of the Auto Pact between the two countries is very important. Rather than replace the Auto Pact, the FTA provides for those parts of the auto industry not covered by it. The FTA allows duty-free import of cars into either country if content meets the 50 percent local production rule (which is based on manufacturing costs) and if the car is produced by one of the carmakers in business in 1965. In practice, the Big Three North American car manufacturers benefit most. The FTA is slightly more restrictive than the old Auto Pact, and its provisions are very similar to those imposed by the European Community on foreign-car production. While it frees up trade between Canada and the United States for North American car production, it discriminates more sharply against virtually all non-North Amer-

Drawing by
Randy Jones

ican car production as well. This is one place where trade diversion probably offsets the benefits of trade creation from the FTA for both countries. By 1996 Canada is also supposed to eliminate the recent practice of giving duty remissions to offshore car companies that locate a production or assembly plant in Canada, such as Hyundai.

Third: The FTA attempts to retain the current market focus and openness of borders that characterize Canada-U.S. energy trade today. The energy trade between Canada and the United States amounted to U.S.$10 billion in 1987 and 1988. Canada is the largest exporter of energy to the United States. The United States supplies 30 percent of Canada's energy imports. Thus two-way trade in energy is important, and the FTA reinforces the efficiency already inherent in this trade.

In brief, neither country can mandate an export price higher than the domestic price; however, private exporters are free to negotiate a higher export price. Similarly, neither country can impose an import tax on energy products from the other country. Virtually all energy forms, including electricity and uranium, are affected by these sweeping provisions. The United States, for example, could not impose an import fee on petroleum without exempting Canada. Rules also exist to provide "entitlements" to "historical shares" during shortages. This agreement goes far toward creating the confidence needed to accelerate drilling and production throughout North America and to allow joint use of facilities such as pipelines and refineries.

Fourth: Continuing earlier reforms by the Mulroney government, foreign investment rules are significantly less restrictive under the FTA. National treatment has virtually become the norm now that discrimination based on nationality is prohibited. (Existing practices that do not conform to the new rules have been permitted to continue, however.) The size threshold for firms subject to scrutiny by Investment Canada (the Canadian foreign investment screening agency) has been raised. Trade-distorting conditions, such as local sourcing requirements and export or import requirements, have been eliminated. In particular, ex post facto rules concerning most indirect investment have been canceled. For example, with few exceptions, a firm selling its operations in the United States cannot now be obligated to sell its Canadian branch to a Canadian bidder. U.S. foreign investment is now far less restricted in Canada, and, conversely, most future Canadian investment in the United States will not be discriminated against.

Fifth: Because of Canadian sensitivity to foreign infringement upon the Canadian identity, the so-called cultural industries were excluded from the negotiations. (Broadcasting, publishing, periodicals and film production fall into this industrial category.) In return, Canada agreed to eliminate some long-standing irritants to Americans in these categories, including tariffs on printed matter and other cultural materials, and the definition of what makes a magazine "Canadian" was changed. The Print in Canada requirement was dropped. It was also agreed that Canada, for the first time, would set up procedures to ensure that U.S. copyright holders were paid for the use of their television programming picked up from U.S. broadcasts and distributed by Canadian cable operators. In general, Canadians left the negotiations knowing that the Canadian identity was not damaged by freer trade but will undoubtedly grow stronger. Should the United States attempt to challenge the cultural provisions, it would be attacking the very foundation of the FTA as far as Canada is concerned.

Sixth: The FTA provides for the most advanced international trade-dispute-resolution mechanism currently feasible inside or outside the provisions of the General Agreement on Tariffs and Trade (GATT). Neither government was genuinely prepared to accept a more formal and binding arrangement. Special binational commissions and panels of experts are to be created from an equal number of Canadians and Americans, plus a chairperson. Chapter 19 of the FTA established separate panels and procedures for antidumping and countervailing duty cases. In general, the procedures come into effect after a request from either Canada or the United States. Domestic routes using established domestic trade institutions, such as the U.S. International Trade Commission or the Canadian International Trade Tribunal, must first be exhausted before the binational route is explored. Domestic law of the importing country applies, although practice and other legal norms could become significant over time as dispute-resolving procedures.

Three major contributions to trade-dispute resolution are the FTA procedures (1) to establish firm timetables for the various steps of the resolution process; (2) to allow foreign nationals to review whether domestic trade law was properly applied and interpreted; and (3) to limit the capacity of either government to enact new trade legislation without at least informing and consulting the other government in advance. These may be regarded as small steps. Binding arbitration, for example, is not required (with some exceptions). Yet these procedures will contribute to the "transparency" and legitimacy of trade decisions on each side of the border in the future. They may also become the model for what is eventually attempted in GATT.

Indirect Benefits of the FTA

In addition to these contributions of the FTA, many smaller innovations may eventually prove to be as salutary as some of the more major changes. For example, there is an effort to make standards and codes in the health and environmental areas more consistent so that these do not become just one more protectionist device. Customs procedures have been reviewed and simplified. Executives moving temporarily back and forth across the border can now do so with a minimum of red tape. Restrictions on financial services in the banking industry have been reduced and future exchanges will be more open, limited only by the pace of domestic reforms in Canada and the United States. In short, binational trade and commerce are likely to proceed more efficiently.

Perhaps the FTA's greatest contribution is the one most overlooked in the debate over ratification. Opponents tended to exaggerate the amount of change that would result; proponents tended to promise more trade benefits than could possibly eventuate. It is well to remember that Canada already conducts nearly 80 percent of its trade with the United States. The FTA is not likely to result in an increase in that share, regardless of the fears of opponents or the promises of proponents. Absolute amounts of trade, of course, may increase substantially. Rather, the FTA will prevent erosion of the level of binational trade that is already quite free. The FTA is an insurance policy against future attempts at protectionism. It is also a step toward making all North American trade more competitive worldwide.

Should this apparently modest goal be regarded as lacking in support, one need only consider the various areas of the agreement. Service provisions do not so much roll back existing restrictions as maintain the current degree of openness. The energy provisions are a statement of the status quo as of 1988-89, a status quo that is far more open than in such previous intervals as 1980–83. Foreign-investment norms approximate the goal of national treatment, nothing more. Dispute-resolution procedures ensure that domestic law will be fairly and efficiently applied: they do not mean that new trade law has been created.

In short, the FTA is a codification of the rules under which Canada and the United States have built a huge international free-trade area since 1945. It contributes to the prosperity of each country. The FTA is a statement to themselves, as much as to the world, that these two countries do not want to see bilateral free trade deteriorate, regardless of the stresses and strains emanating from the world trading system in the future. To some, this is an all-too-modest statement. In fact, it is a very ambitious and encompassing guarantee that few nations in the past, over long periods, have ever been able to achieve. The FTA is a victory for the retention of the best that the economic marketplace has yet been able to provide in North America.

Defense Policy After the Mulroney White Paper

At the core of the original Mulroney defense policy was the proposal of Defense Minister Perrin Beatty that Canada acquire 10 to 12 nuclear-powered submarines for long-range ocean surveillance and control operations in the Arctic as well as the Atlantic and Pacific. Uncontroversial as this proposal may seem, it stirred up defense thinking in a way that nothing else had since the Trudeau government's controversial decision to halve the size of the Canadian deployment of NATO troops. On the one hand, some Canadians and foreign allies liked the proposal. Many Canadians believed it would help secure their sovereignty in the Arctic North. As mentioned earlier, U.S. ships had twice demonstrated that the Northwest Passage was navigable, to which efforts Canadians had reacted negatively by expanding their territorial claims to the Arctic region. As nuclear-powered submarines could patrol these waters under ice and operate nearly undetected for long periods, they seemed just the vehicle to keep tabs on the Russians (if they were so foolish as to test the ice canyons and shallows of the Arctic expanses) and perhaps the Americans and British, who undoubtedly were out there guarding against Russian subs as well.

Many of Canada's allies liked the proposal insofar as it would commit Canada to leave its free-rider status of a little more than 2 percent of its GNP for defense and spend an amount more in keeping with its wealth and status. The Mulroney government's estimate of the cost—including maintenance, training, and command and control—was on the order of C$8 billion (U.S.$6.5 billion), probably a conservative estimate despite the fact that payment would be spread over 10 or more years.

On the other side of this issue there were many doubters. As one high-ranking member of the Department of Finance remarked prior to November 1988, "I think we should talk about this issue, and talk about it, and talk about it right up through the federal election." He did <u>not</u> say that Ottawa should ever actually buy the subs. For many Canadians, the subs looked too expensive. They would tilt the budget of the Department of National Defense toward the navy.

Foreigners too had their doubts. First, they were concerned that Canada would not be able to match the job done by the British and the Americans, because it would have to cut corners in terms of submarine size, quality and ultimately numbers. Much of this concern was sheer petty nationalism. The U.S. Navy did not want competition, and both Britain and the United States preferred the notion of a two-member club, even though the territory being patrolled was Canadian.

Second, given rapid technological change, it was not clear that submarines would continue to be the best means of tracking other submarines or that the small subs Canada wanted to buy would at the time of purchase contain state-of-the-art technology. Without such technology, the small Canadian submarine would never be able to hunt down an advanced Soviet submarine.

Third, a suspicion arose among Canada's allies that the effect of the submarine decision would be to force Canada out of Europe. The defense budget was simply not large enough to do all things at the same time, and the first large item to go would be the cost of European troops. A gradual "hollowing out" of the European defense commitment was feared.

From the Canadian perspective these concerns were patronizing and perhaps irrelevant. It was, after all, Canadian territory that Ottawa was considering patrolling. It was Canadian dollars that would be spent, not allied monies. Respected Canadian analysts also contended—and this worried NATO defense experts most of all—that the question of Canadian withdrawal from Europe was a nonissue because by the year 2000 the United States, too, would be out of Europe. Why pick on Canada now, they challenged, when the brunt of its decision would not be felt until the year 2000?

The circus-like atmosphere of the submarine decision played itself out as the White House, by virtue of a turbulent top-level decision, promised Canada full support in obtaining the necessary technology to build and operate the submarines. Next, the allies gave their blessing and encouraged Canada to proceed. Yet the subsequent decision of the Mulroney government first to go slow on and then to junk the submarine idea for reasons of cost (presaged by Beatty's appointment to the national health and welfare portfolio in the cabinet) made all of the debate irrelevant. Nevertheless, the controversy signaled two important developments central to the broader defense debate among the allies. Not only had the issue of burden-sharing and defense coordination heated up in a significant way, but the allies were beginning to measure their own sovereignty needs against the needs of collective security.

For no other country in the alliance would this trade-off between national sovereignty, on the one hand, and collective alliance strength, on the other, be more pressing than for Canada. Canada needs NATO Europe as a political counterweight to U.S. preponderance. The difficulty posed by this trade-off would preoccupy NATO in the Gorbachev era. Canada's initiatives and analysis were only bringing to the "front burner" what other allies were attempting to keep on the back. Furthermore, national sovereignty, continentalism, and Pacific and North Atlantic security all were beginning to fall into different analytic compartments. Future defense thinking will have to bring all of these separate compartments back together into a single construct. Overall alliance leadership will not get any easier.

Acid Rain and the Environment

Throughout the 1980s one environmental issue dominated the bilateral diplomatic agenda—acid rain. Evidence of the damage acid rain has caused to the physical environment and to human health has continued to accumulate. It shows that acid rain has sterilized lakes and killed fish; defaced public statues and the exteriors of buildings; stunted the growth of many types of trees and begun to decimate spruce forests; and contributed to lung disease, albeit less immediately than cigarettes and emissions from leaded gasoline. Although Canada pressed hard for measures for acid-rain cleanup, such action has been slow to emerge.

Lack of progress in the talks on acid rain derives, first of all, from the nature of the problem: acid rain is virtually invisible and its effects occur only after long periods. Incremental problems seldom lead to rapid policy action in a democracy, because it is easier to postpone a decision when there is no crisis to threaten or otherwise embarrass the decisionmaker. Moreover, competing interests, such as the desire to eliminate toxic dumps, may claim a disproportionate amount of public and therefore congressional support. This is, of course, what happened on the U.S. side.

Conflicting interests, particularly between producer and recipient, have also interfered with progress in eliminating acid rain. The producer has always been larger and more powerful than the recipient. Since the damage typically occurs at a distance from where the acid rain is actually produced, and the cost of cleanup is large, the producer has little incentive to change his ways. Although Canada produces substantial amounts of acid rain, a disproportionate amount of the acid rain that falls on Quebec, parts of Ontario and the Maritime Provinces comes from the United States. In the United States, New England produces some acid rain but less than it receives. The principal source of New England's pollution is the Midwest.

Although the United States was long excoriated for temporizing by insisting on additional research, it was legitimately difficult to identify correctly the cause and effect of acid rain. Initially, Canada thought, as did most other governments anxious to proceed with cleanup, that the problem originated with the sulfur oxides alone. These were mainly produced by fixed-point sources, such as the coal-fired utilities in Ohio and the smelters in Ontario. Research eventually demonstrated what many chemists had long suspected. Sulfur oxides mixed with dust particles acted simultaneously with the nitrogen oxides. The resulting deposits involved both sulfur and nitric acids, a caustic brew much more damaging than its individual components. The findings meant that both the fixed-point sources and the moving sources—such as automobiles, which produce the nitrogen oxides—are responsible for the environmental damage. The policy problem was thus much broader than originally thought, and more difficult to resolve.

Fortunately, the Bush Administration moved early in its first weeks in office to advance the cause of acid-rain cleanup. The particular political twist that was necessary to achieve progress is worthy of notice. In order to obtain an American solution, the Bush Administration had to characterize acid rain as an "American problem." This strategy holds many implications for how irritants are to be resolved in a relationship as complicated and interdependent as that of Canada and the United States. U.S. opponents of expenditures on acid-rain cleanup often sought to delay action by attributing concern about acid rain only to Canadians (foreigners do not vote for U.S. congressmen!), and then in pejorative terms that implied Canadians really only wanted to sell more clean natural gas and hydropower to the United States as a substitute for dirty Appalachian coal. This tactic was countered by the argument that acid rain was largely an American problem, with the damage occurring inside U.S. borders. Canada thus learned that to work the relationship with the United States to its own advantage, low profile was sometimes the best route to bilateral policy success.

In Conclusion

Although on an individual basis Canadians and Americans may sometimes be indistinguishable, on the statistical basis of large numbers, the differences are profound. These differences are likely to remain, regardless of free-trade areas or joint defense policies. Moreover, each country cherishes these differences in political institutions and social values. Quebec merely accentuates the complex diversity that is Canada and that distinguishes Canada from the United States.

Unity in diversity is a compelling political theme in a modern pluralist democracy. But the greater the diversity, at least insofar as large, homogeneous, regional, ethnic and cultural blocs are concerned, the greater the potential for less unity, as well. As the debate over the Meech Lake accord revealed, Canada is continually in the process of redefining the relationship between the federal government and the provinces, and between the peripheral regions and the Ontario center. Americans should not be surprised if the psychological aspects of these debates sometimes spill over onto them, especially when they themselves are partner to an agreement as vast as the formal establishment of a free-trade area. Anti-Americanism, insofar as it can be said to exist in Canada, is sometimes politically useful because it serves to hold together what have been called the "warring duchies."

Canada and the United States were the model for the original notion of "political interdependence," a notion that will always look more appealing to the larger partner. Yet the benefits of political interdependence are undeniably shared. The very high economic growth rate of Canada in the post-1945 period, second only to Japan among OECD (Organization for Economic Cooperation and Development) countries, attests to these benefits. But the psychological relationship is for Americans most important to master. They must recognize, for example, that if by word or deed they impugn the Canadian identity, they will reap exactly the animosity that most Americans would dearly love to suppress.

Americans tend to rank Canada as their "friendliest neighbor." Canadians, by their buying preferences and travel habits, admit that the United States is a unique partner. When the two governments have problems "managing the relationship," public opinion on each side of the border eventually forces the governments to resolve their differences. The true magic of Canada-U.S. relations is that through vigilance and diligence, the two countries have learned to share a continent without losing mutual respect.

Talking It Over

A Note for Students and Discussion Groups

This issue of the HEADLINE SERIES, like its predecessors, is published for every serious reader, specialized or not, who takes an interest in the subject. Many of our readers will be in classrooms, seminars or community discussion groups. Particularly with them in mind, we present below some discussion questions—suggested as a starting point only—and references for further reading.

Discussion Questions

It has been said that an external threat contributes to the unification of a country. Discuss Canada's evolution to national unity.

How and why was confederation achieved in 1867?

What were the problems the British North America Act sought to resolve? How successfully did it do so?

What was the "national policy," and how was it developed under Macdonald and Laurier?

Canadian history can best be understood by examining three interlocking relationships: Canada and the United States, Canada and the provinces, and English and French Canada. Discuss.

Should Quebec have a special status in the Canadian federation?

It has sometimes been argued that the best way to solve federal-provincial strains is to decentralize—that is, to give increased powers to all the provinces. The Meech Lake accord called for increased decentralization. Is this a practicable arrangement for contemporary Canada?

How significant is the role of party ideology in both the federal and provincial governments? What are the ideological distinctions of the three major political parties in Canada?

To what extent do economic and cultural factors affect or determine federal-provincial relations?

Identify the most important events in Canada's evolution as an international actor prior to World War II, and discuss their significance.

Show how Canada, as a "middle power," has participated in multilateral organizations and played a significant and distinctive international role.

Some have argued that there is a remarkable continuity in Canada's international role; others have argued to the contrary. Discuss, with special emphasis on whether you think Canadian foreign policy objectives have changed since World War II.

Why does the United States seem to take Canada for granted? Does it in fact do so?

Is Canada able to devise an "independent" foreign policy, given its interdependence with the United States? How does this relationship fit into Canada's overall range of relations with other regions and countries?

What alternatives does Canada have to an increasingly close economic relationship with the United States, especially in the wake of the Free Trade Agreement?

READING LIST

Bothwell, Robert, Drummond, Ian, and English, John, *Canada Since 1945: Power, Politics, and Provincialism.* Toronto, University of Toronto Press, 1981. Provides a comprehensive account of Canada from 1945 to the beginning of the 1980s.

Brown, Craig, *Canada's National Policy, 1883–1900: A Study in Canadian American Relations.* Princeton, N.J., Princeton University Press, 1964. Considers the "national policy" in a historical and international context.

Brown, R. C., and Cook, R., *Canada: 1896–1921: A Nation Transformed.* Toronto, McClelland & Stewart, 1974. Provides an overview of immigration to western Canada and the war years.

"Canada." *Current History,* March 1988 (entire issue). Focuses on "the impact the Free Trade Agreement with the United States will have on . . . diverse areas of Canadian society."

Clarkson, Stephen, ed., *An Independent Foreign Policy for Canada?* Toronto, McClelland & Stewart, 1968. Addresses the alleged uncritical acceptance of the U.S. view of the world in Canada's foreign policy.

Diebold, William, Jr., ed., *Bilateralism, Multilateralism and Canada in U.S. Trade Policy.* Cambridge, Mass., Ballinger Publishing Co. for the Council on Foreign Relations, 1988. Five experts from the United States, Canada and Mexico examine the critical issues raised by the U.S.-Canada free-trade agreement.

Doran, Charles F., *Forgotten Partnership: U.S.-Canada Relations Today.* Baltimore, Md., The Johns Hopkins University Press, 1984. Examines all aspects of this bilateral relationship.

Eayrs, James, *In Defence of Canada,* Vol. II, *Appeasement and Rearmament.* Toronto, University of Toronto Press, 1965. An exhaustive analysis of Canadian foreign policy in the late 1930s.

Eccles, W. J., *The Canadian Frontier, 1534–1760.* Albuquerque, University of New Mexico Press, 1965. Describes the origins of the French Canadians.

Fox, Paul W., and White, Graham, eds., *Politics: Canada.* Toronto, McGraw-Hill Ryerson Ltd., 1987. Provides an excellent review of domestic political institutions.

Glazebrook, G. P. de Twenebroker, *A History of Canadian External Relations.* Toronto, McClelland & Stewart, 1966. Provides good background reading.

Holmes, J. W., *Life with Uncle: The Canadian-American Relationship.* Toronto, University of Toronto Press, 1981. Deals with the critical question of Canadian-American relations in the postwar years.

———, *The Shaping of Peace,* Vol. II. Toronto, University of Toronto Press, 1982. Provides a good account of Canada's role in the formation of NATO.

Jockel, J., *No Boundaries Upstairs.* Vancouver, University of British Columbia Press, 1987. Traces the origins of Norad.

———, and Sokolsky, J., *Canada and Collective Security.* Washington, D.C., Praeger, 1987. Looks at Canada's role in collective security and discusses what more Canada can do.

Kirton, J., and de Witt, A., *Canada as a Principal Power: A Study in Foreign Policy and International Relations.* Toronto, John Wiley & Sons, 1983. Exhaustively examines how Canada has taken successful initiatives with regard to various international issues.

Matheson, W. A., *The Prime Minister and the Cabinet.* Toronto, Methuen Publications, 1976. Clearly discusses the role of the prime minister and the cabinet.

Neatby, H. B., *The Politics of Chaos in the Thirties.* Toronto, Macmillan, 1972. Deals with prime ministership of William Lyon Mackenzie King, Canada's longest-governing prime minister.

Sager, E., Fischer, L., and Pierson, S., eds., *From Atlantic Canada and Confederation: Essays in Canadian Political Economy.* Toronto, University of Toronto Press, 1983. Discusses the various aspects of regionalism.

Smith, Goldwin, *Canada and the Canadian Question* (1891), reprinted in the *Social History of Canada* series. Toronto, University of Toronto Press, 1971. Classic view of Canadian regionalism.

Stacey, C. P., *Canada & the Age of Conflict: A History of Canadian External Policies,* Vol. II, *1921–1948: The Mackenzie King Era.* Toronto, University of Toronto Press, 1981. Provides an overview of the interwar years.

Thorburn, Hugh G., ed., *Party Politics in Canada.* Toronto, Prentice Hall Canada Inc., 1985. Examines all aspects of party politics in Canada.

Wade, Mason, *The French Canadians,* Vol. I. Toronto, Macmillan, 1977. Focuses on the question of Canadian duality.

Wonnacott, Paul, *The United States and Canada: The Quest for Free Trade.* Washington, D.C., The Institute for International Economics, 1987. Analyzes the different issues and difficulties of free trade.

Footnotes

1. *Challenge and Commitment: A Defence Policy for Canada* (Ottawa, Department of Supply and Services, 1987).
2. John Dales, "Protection, Immigration and Canadian Nationality," in John Dales, ed., *Nationalism in Canada* (Toronto, Holt Rinehart and Winston, 1966), pp. 167–70.
3. Robert Bothwell, Ian Drummond, John English, *Canada Since 1945: Power, Politics, and Provincialism* (Toronto, University of Toronto Press, 1981), p. 132.
4. Ibid., p. 247.
5. Ibid., p. 258.
6. Ibid., p. 289.
7. *Foreign Policy for Canadians* (Ottawa, Department of Supply and Services, 1970).
8. Bothwell, Drummond, English, *op. cit.,* p. 363.
9. W.A. Matheson, *The Prime Minister and the Cabinet* (Toronto, Methuen Publications, 1976), passim.
10. Hugh G. Thorburn, ed., *Party Politics in Canada* (Toronto, Prentice Hall Canada, 1985).
11. Ibid., p. 98.